Midnight Math

Twelve Terrific Math Games

Peter
Ledwon
and
Marilyn
Mets

Holiday House/New York

Library of Congress Cataloging-in-Publication Data
Ledwon, Peter.
Midnight math: twelve terrific math games/
by Peter Ledwon; illustrated by Marilyn Mets.
p. cm.
Summary: Animal characters help readers play twelve
different math games.
ISBN 0-8234-1530-9
1. Mathematical recreations—Juvenile literature.
[1. Mathematical recreations.] I. Mets, Marilyn, ill.
II. Title.
QA95 .L42 2000
793.7'4—dc21   99-037167

Here We Go!

Tick, tock.
The hands
on the clock
wish they were feet
so they could run,
as Chester, Leon,
and Maury
get ready
for midnight fun.

Star

The sky is
full of sparkling
jewels. White
ones, blue ones,
orange ones,
pink ones,
green ones,
yellow ones.

Can you count
all the stars?

Search

Play this game by counting stars. How many white stars are there? How many blue stars? How many orange stars?

Each color of star has a different number of points. The green star has seven points. How many points does the pink star have?

Treasure Blast!

Everything flew out of the treasure box when the table tipped! Help Leon, Chester, and Maury put it all back using this list.

10

9

8

7

6

5

4

3

2

1

Hot Salsa!

You be Maury. Let your friend be Chester!

If all 6 chips are found in 3 minutes, Maury and Chester trade places. If not, they play the same way again!

Snack Attack!

Keep Chester, Maury, and Leon
well fed tonight.
Count the snacks!
How many are there?

 More
than
one?

 Less
than
three?

 More
than
two?

 Less
than
four?

More
than
three?

Less
than
five?

 More
than
four?

 Less
than
six?

 More
than
five?

Less
than
seven?

How many other things
can you see?

Crackers Jack

WATCH OUT! Polly really, really likes this game.

Shuffle the cards. Deal them all out.

Keep the cards face down.

Chester goes first.

So I turn my top card over...

... and put it on the table.

All players take turns.

They keep playing until somebody turns over a jack.

LOOK! Chester turns over a jack!

The first person to shout "Crackers Jack!" slaps his or her hand on the jack, and keeps all the cards underneath.

They keep playing.
Oops, Leon makes a mistake.
Crackers JACK!
not a jack
Now Leon must give each of the other players a card from his stack.
Now I've got more cards than Leon!
When you run out of cards you're out of the game. The last person with cards is the winner.

Something Fishy

To begin,
shuffle the cards.
One player deals.
Each player gets
five cards.

16

The rest of the cards go in the middle. This is the fish pond.

Put your cards in order—from small numbers to big numbers. Don't let anyone see them. These are Leon's cards.

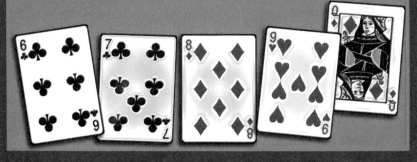

Try to collect two cards with the same number. Like sevens! When you get two cards with the same number you have a "pair."

Put your pairs face up on the table only when it's your turn.

If you don't have a pair, ask another player for a card you need to make a pair. If the player doesn't have one, try the fish pond.

No, Leon. Go fish.

Chester, do you have any sevens?

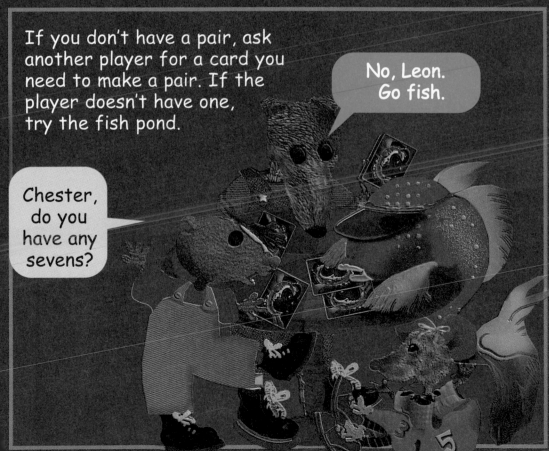

Yikes! Leon got a seven from the pond.

Leon's hand looks like this with the pair of sevens. He puts them on the table.

Now it's Chester's turn.

a pair

Bubbles, do you have a six card?

No, Chester. Go fish!

Leon will be right back.

They play and play.

Leon has put all his pairs on the table. Oops, he has no cards left.

Who is the winner this time?

Chester

Each card is 1 point.

Chester has 2 pairs. 2+2=4

I'm tied with Chester.

Leon

Leon has 2 pairs also. 2+2=4

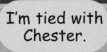

Jumpin' Jack flash!

I WIN!

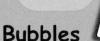

Bubbles

Bubble has 3 pairs. 2+2+2=6

Still fishing for the right answer? Try Leon's handy-dandy calculator. Here's how:

If your question is 4+7=?, first find 4 in the green column. Put a finger on the square and run it across the row.

+	1
1	2
2	3
3	4
4	→

Next, find 7 in the blue column. Put another finger on that square. Run your finger up and down the column.

7	8
↓	9
9	10
10	11

The square where your two fingers meet is the answer.

Leon's Amazing Calculator

+	1	2	3	4	5	6	7	8	9	10
1	2	3	4	5	6	7	8	9	10	11
2	3	4	5	6	7	8	9	10	11	12
3	4	5	6	7	8	9	10	11	12	13
4	5	6	7	8	9	10	11	12	13	14
5	6	7	8	9	10	11	12	13	14	15
6	7	8	9	10	11	12	13	14	15	16
7	8	9	10	11	12	13	14	15	16	17
8	9	10	11	12	13	14	15	16	17	18
9	10	11	12	13	14	15	16	17	18	19
10	11	12	13	14	15	16	17	18	19	20

Shuffle Off!

Make a big game board like the one in the next square.

Use paper or chalk on the floor.

Take turns. You toss your marker onto the board.

Add up all your points.

If a marker, like my button, lands off the board you get 0 points.

I got a 6. It's Chester's turn!

I got a 4! Your turn, Leon!

Keep adding and taking turns.

The first person to reach 20 points wins!

This time I got a 1! 1+6=7

Dicey Pairs

Leon! Toss 1 die so we can start!

Roll down the stairs!
- Fun for 2 or more players
- Play with 2 or more dice (more dice is easier)

- Toss 1 die first. This Is how many tries each player gets to throw dicey pairs at his turn.

I can only find 3 dice. Today we will play with 3.

I'm tossing a die, Chester! Heads up.

Boink!

Two! We have 2 tries each to throw dicey pairs.

Me first! Come on, gimme a pair!

NOPE, no pair on this try, Chester. Toss again.

Hurry up! I'm next.

TOSS!

WHOOSH! CLATTER!

Look, Chester has a pair of ones on his second try.

He DID it!

NO Way!

It's his turn AGAIN.

Now I get 2 tries to throw another dicey pair.

Oh no! I missed both tries. Since I'm so great, you guys are going to gimme another turn, right?

No way! It's my turn to try for dicey pairs.

I'm on a roll. How do I win this game?

Throw all six dicey pairs to win.

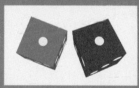

Hand the dice back to the master. I'll show you how.

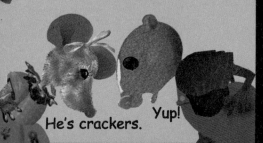

He's crackers. Yup!

Gee whiz! Some people have no sense of humor.

23

Nasty Pirate Treasure Hunt

Collect 9 pieces of awesome treasure. We've got 3 spiders + 3 buttons + 3 pieces of gums.

Pick a captain! I pick Leon.

Okay!

Captain Leon hides all the treasure.

Then he calls the crew to find it.

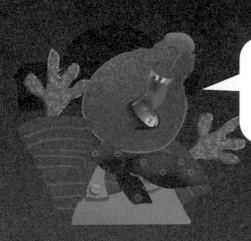

Ahoy, mates! I hid all the treasures. Now find them quick.

One piece found, Captain Leon!

How many left, Captain Leon?

GULP!

We had 3 pieces to start. 3-1=2 pieces left. Keep looking, mates.

Two spiders, Captain!

How many left?

TWO? WRONG! 3-2=1

Now I'm Captain!

I'm tired of all this mutiny.

Let's play something else.

25

Looney Hopscotch

This game will keep you hopping!

Get Ready –
- With chalk or tape make a gameboard like the one on the next page.
- Find something to toss.
- Pick who goes first.

I go first. I have to toss my lucky button onto 1. If I miss it's Leon's turn.

Yes!

Jump over 1 and land on 2. I GET IT!

A two-foot landing.

Two is an even number like 4, 6, and 8. You land on both feet on even numbers.

Three is an odd number like 1, 5, and 7. You land on one foot on odd numbers.

Hop to 3.

One foot

Maury keeps going to number 8. Then she turns around and goes back to 2.

She picks up the button.

I jump off the board and toss my button onto 2. If I miss it's Leon's turn.

26

How to Win

The first person to get a marker onto 8 wins.

Lose a turn when:
· your toss misses
· you hop instead of jump.

Uh-oh, sun's coming up. Only time for one more game.

Start

Jack's Back

(Too bad Jack's a loser. Let's hope he's a good sport.)

Keep this one!

Hey guys! Help me find all four jacks in the deck. We only need 1 jack for this game. Let's keep the jack of clubs.

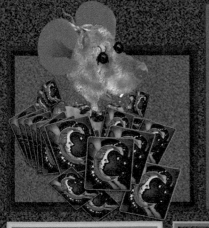

Maury deals all of the cards to the others. Some players will have more cards.

Everyone sorts their cards.

Anytime a player has two cards with the same number, that pair is put face down on the table.

Maury is going first. She turns to Leon, the player on her left. Without seeing the fronts of his cards, she picks one from his hand.

Great! I got a 2 from Leon. Now I've got a pair. I'll put them on the table.

All players take turns, taking a card from the player on their left.

They all hope they can make a pair.

Please take my jack.

No jack. No jack.

Rats! Jack!

YESSS!!

I hope Maury picks the jack now. I don't want to get stuck with it.

The game keeps going until everyone runs out of cards.

Well, almost everyone.

Someone is going to be left holding that one jack.

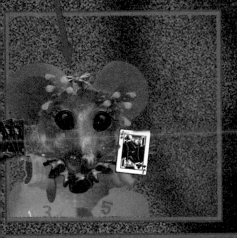

That player, unfortunately, is the game's Grand Prize Loser. All of the other players get to point and shout, "Jack's the loser!"

Yikes! I'm outta here!

Sunrise Coming

Dark sky turned a brilliant red,

The clouds began to light.

Bright winks peeked around the sun,

Time to grab the toys and run.

Did You Know?

MIDNIGHT MATH Answers Page

Star Search (pages 6 and 7):
Did you count a total of 45 stars? There are 12 cream stars, 10 orange stars, 8 pink stars, 6 green stars, 5 yellow stars, and 4 blue stars.

Snack Attack! (pages 12 and 13):
All those yummy snacks. How many did you see? There are 2 pizza slices, 3 cherries, 4 slices of toast, 5 muffins, and 6 bananas. There is a total of 20 snacks.

More Games To Try:
You can make up your own new games. Here are some ideas: Did you notice that the numbers on Maury's dress keep changing? Add up the numbers on each dress. Then add up all the numbers on each page.

You can find all kinds of things to count and add up in your home, classroom, or neighborhood, such as windows, shoes, pockets, mailboxes, and red cars.

Star Search (pages 6 and 7):
Make up counting games using the number of points on the stars. Add up the number of points on one blue star and one red star. Then add up the number of points on one yellow star and one green star. Which is more, the number of blue and red points added together or the number of yellow and green points added?

Something Fishy (pages 16, 17, and 18)
Try playing this game with only the numbered cards. Remove all the face cards, then deal 5 cards to each player. Instead of collecting pairs of cards that match, collect groups of cards that add up to 10. For example, 3 and 7 would make a group. 5 and 2 and 3 would make another. When all the cards are used up or no other groups can be made with the remaining cards, the game is over. The player with the most cards wins.

Shuffle Off! (pages 20 and 21)
You can also play Shuffle Off! backward. Each player begins with 20 points. Every time a player's marker lands on a number, subtract that number. If a player gets 4 on his or her first turn then subtract 4 from 20 to get the new score: 20 4=16. The first player to reach 0 wins. Negative scores are not allowed. If a player has 1 point left, but lands on 3, he or she must wait until the next turn to try to land on a 1.

Whether you're playing the games in this book or games you invented yourself, don't forget to have fun!